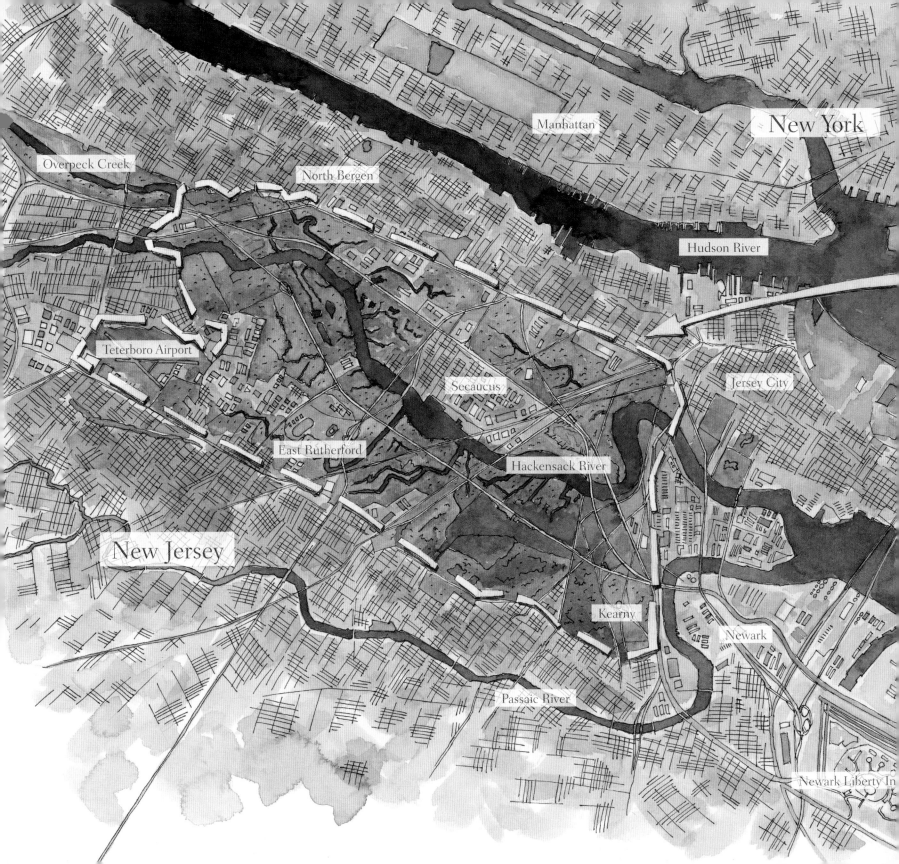

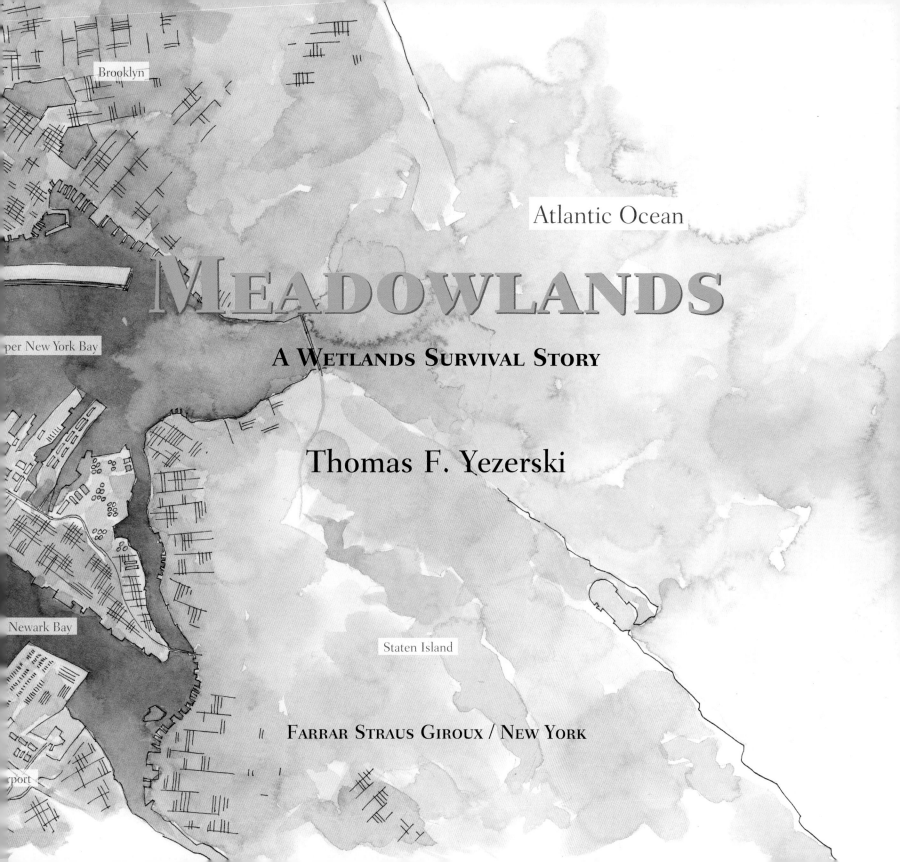

Brooklyn

Atlantic Ocean

MEADOWLANDS

A WETLANDS SURVIVAL STORY

per New York Bay

Thomas F. Yezerski

Newark Bay

Staten Island

FARRAR STRAUS GIROUX / NEW YORK

rport

To Eleni

Thanks to Hugh Carola from Hackensack Riverkeeper
and to the New Jersey Meadowlands Commission for their review and assistance

Copyright © 2011 by Thomas F. Yezerski
All rights reserved
Distributed in Canada by D&M Publishers, Inc.
Color separations by Embassy Graphics
Printed in November 2010 in China
by Imago, Shenzen, Guangdong Province
Designed by Jay Colvin
First edition, 2011
1   3   5   7   9   10   8   6   4   2

www.fsgkidsbooks.com

Library of Congress Cataloging-in-Publication Data
Yezerski, Thomas.
    Meadowlands: a wetlands survival story / Thomas F. Yezerski.— 1st ed.
       p.   cm.
    Includes bibliographical references and index.
    ISBN: 978-0-374-34913-4 (alk. paper)
    1. Wetland ecology—New Jersey—Hackensack Meadowlands.   2. Wetland
conservation—New Jersey—Hackensack Meadowlands.   3. Hackensack Meadowlands
(N.J.)—Description and travel.   I. Title.

QH105.N5Y49 2011
577.6909749'2—dc22
                                                                                2010005503

New Jersey Turnpike

mall

warehouse

weeds

parking lot

garbage dump

mobsters

mosquitoes

swamps

From the top of the Empire State Building in New York City, you can see a flat, wet place in New Jersey. Some people think it's just smelly swamps. Others think of it as where the airport or malls or stadiums are. Most people think it's not much of a place at all. This place is called the Meadowlands.

Teterboro Airport

football fans

rest stop

chemical dump

racetrack

pottery vessel

white-tailed deer

corn cake

rock knife

osprey

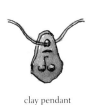
clay pendant

The Meadowlands is an estuary where the Hackensack River empties into Newark Bay. Much of it is wetlands, with a mix of freshwater and salt water soaking the spongy ground. When the Atlantic Ocean tide comes in, parts of the wetlands are underwater. Hundreds of years ago, the Meadowlands was 20,000 acres of marshes, swamps, and bogs that were home to many different plants and animals.

maize

cornhusk doll

strawberry

black bear

sunflower

bog turtle

mayapple

dugout canoe

squash

turkey

Humans lived there, too. The wetlands supported the Lenni Lenape for thousands of years. They built wigwams on the surrounding dry upland. They fished in canoes, with nets. They dug oysters out of the mud. With bows and arrows, they hunted ducks, rabbits, and other animals. They gathered many kinds of nuts, roots, and berries.

moccasin

oyster

chestnut

passenger pigeon

house

wampum

knife

horse

scythe

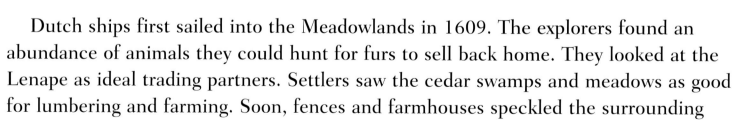
shallop

Dutch ships first sailed into the Meadowlands in 1609. The explorers found an abundance of animals they could hunt for furs to sell back home. They looked at the Lenape as ideal trading partners. Settlers saw the cedar swamps and meadows as good for lumbering and farming. Soon, fences and farmhouses speckled the surrounding hillsides.

musket

cow

Conestoga wagon

muskrat

bridge

barn

duffel cloth

ferry

fur hat

windmill

Through the 1800s, loggers cut down the Meadowlands' trees. Farmers dug ditches to drain the land of excess water and filled marshes with dirt to add to their property. They laid wood-planked roads through the Meadowlands to get to New York–bound ferries. Many Lenape died of diseases brought by the European settlers, and the rest were forced to move away.

kettle

trap

Half Moon

haystack

Interstate 80

hangers

cargo plane

sport-utility vehicle

freezer truck

pesticide

By the mid-twentieth century, the Meadowlands had been diked, dammed, and drained to control mosquitoes and drinking water. Plank roads had become highways, railways, and runways. Trucks and trains crossed the Meadowlands to ship goods from ports on Newark Bay and the Hackensack River. More and more people came to New York City by car on the highways and by plane through Newark Airport.

commuter bus

chocolate drink

fresh-air scent

concrete blocks

forest-green dye

freight train

vitamin C

Pulaski Skyway

benzene

container truck

drawbridge

passenger jet

candy wrappers

zippers

Industries dug into the wetlands to be close to the rivers and rails that brought raw materials in and delivered finished products to customers. They set up factories there to build new inventions. Their refineries turned oil into gasoline and plastic. Power plants burned coal to generate electricity. Laboratories created chemicals to flavor our food and color our clothes.

meal containers

dioxins

concrete block

hydrocarbons

mercury

electronic game

People working in the Meadowlands and living nearby used the wetlands as a wasteland. Factories poured chemicals into the Hackensack River. Towns along the river poured sewage into it and dumped garbage into the marshes. Cars, trucks, planes, and the factories blew smoke into the air.

coal ash

hexavalent chromium

candy wrapper

sludge

mobster

methane

old Penn Station column

diesel exhaust

batteries

leachate

The garbage dumps grew into trash mountains. Methane gas from the trash exploded and burned. Creeks turned poisonous, and the wind smelled like paint. Fish and birds fled to find better places to live. Plants withered. By the 1960s, there were only 11,000 acres of wetlands left in the Meadowlands.

luxury sedan

polychlorinated biphenyl

arrowhead

videotape

hardware store

trash cans

cement mixer

condominium

shrubs

crane

The Meadowlands had deteriorated into one of the worst places in America, and it was giving New Jersey a bad reputation. The state government decided to turn the wasteland into a center for housing, shopping, and entertainment, while protecting parts of the wetlands. In 1969, the state began to close the landfills and stop chemical dumping.

office building

forklift

motorboat

tennis court

restaurant

steamroller

office supply store

shopping cart

gazebo

hotel

Once the region started looking and smelling better, developers moved in. They covered the landfills and more wetlands with dirt and debris. On top of that, they built big stores, giant stadiums, houses, and apartments. In 1985, there were less than 7,000 acres of wetlands left in the Meadowlands.

delivery truck

bookstore

gas station

Dumpster

pale corydalis

salt-marsh cordgrass

tree of heaven

phytoplankton

marsh thistle

redtop grass

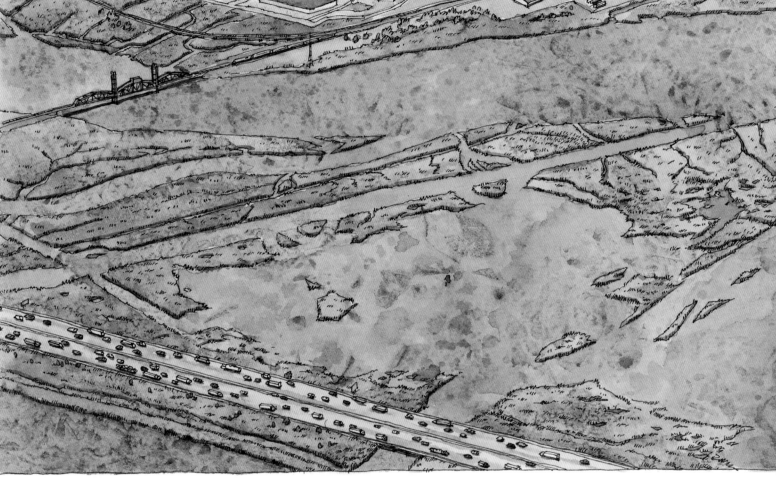

But even after being dug out, filled in, run over, and dumped on, the wetlands still showed signs of life. The Hackensack River still flowed south. The tide still rose north from the Atlantic Ocean. The river and tide still met in the Meadowlands twice a day, as they had for 10,000 years. Because they did, the ecosystem had a chance to recover.

scrub oak

common reed

swamp rose mallow

mugwort

beardtongue

smooth cordgrass

purple loosestrife

Himalayan blackberry

bluejoint

starry campion

All along, the river carried little bits of dirt and dead plants, called detritus, from the hills. The tide brought little bits of plankton and algae from the Atlantic Ocean. As they pushed against each other and slowed down, the river and tide dropped their bits to the bottom of the marsh. Fresh muck piled up every day.

princess tree

goldenrod

pennywort

narrow-leaf cattail

aurora damsel

whirligig beetle

American lady

swamp mosquito

caddisworm

greenhead fly

When chemical dumping stopped, the muck could slowly filter pollution out of the water and bury it under layers of new muck. Nutrients in the new muck could then feed seeds carried by the river, tide, and wind. The seeds grew into grasses and reeds, which also helped to filter chemicals from the water.

black swallowtail

lady beetle

twelve-spotted skimmer

water flea

eastern pondhawk

coffee bean snail

house mosquito

backswimmer

mayfly

zooplankton

Less pollution also meant the swirling freshwater and salt water had more oxygen to add to the little bits of plankton, algae, and detritus. The oxygen helped bacteria in the water break down the mix into a nutritious soup for snails, worms, and insects. The reeds rattled and ticked, and the wetlands buzzed with millions of bugs.

bloodworm

salt-marsh mosquito

grass shrimp

cabbage white

American eel

white perch

striped bass

Atlantic butterfish

common carp

bluegill

The river and tide helped heal the Meadowlands, slowly filtering out poisonous chemicals, absorbing oxygen, and feeding plants and microorganisms. Tough little mummichogs survived the worst pollution, and now they have cleaner water and more small prey to eat.

Atlantic tomcod

weakfish

winter flounder

red hake

blueback herring

Atlantic sturgeon

menhaden

pumpkinseed

hogchoker

alewife

Healthy populations of small fish attract bigger fish, which come from the cold ocean during high tide to hunt the small fish and to lay their eggs in the warmer, calmer marsh water. Among the cozy grasses, their young are safer from the even bigger fish that might eat them in the ocean. When they have grown old enough, they ride the river current back to sea.

spotfin killifish

Atlantic silverside

American shad

black sea bass

mud turtle

meadow vole

Fowler's toad

northern water snake

muskrat

blue crab

When the tide starts to fall again, the river and creeks begin to shrink. Fish must flee to deep water or they will be trapped in shallow puddles. The falling tide is also like a rising curtain, exposing the muddy banks of the river and creeks and revealing more creatures that are thriving again in the Meadowlands. This is the chance for the fiddler crabs to dance.

painted turtle

eastern milk snake

diamondback terrapin

southern leopard frog

mud crab

green frog

brown snake

red-eared slider

box turtle

brown rat

Each male fiddler has one big clumsy claw he waves back and forth, back and forth. He taps his pointy feet so quietly, only a female fiddler crab can hear him. If she likes his performance, she will follow him home to his burrow in the mud. The waterline flickers with rows of hundreds of yellow claws.

garter snake

red fox

pickerel frog

snapping turtle

red-winged blackbird

black skimmer

spotted sandpiper

starling

sedge wren

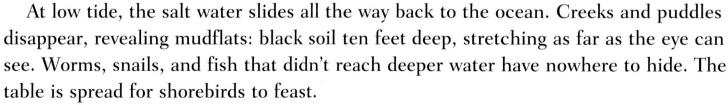

black tern

At low tide, the salt water slides all the way back to the ocean. Creeks and puddles disappear, revealing mudflats: black soil ten feet deep, stretching as far as the eye can see. Worms, snails, and fish that didn't reach deeper water have nowhere to hide. The table is spread for shorebirds to feast.

clapper rail

Forster's tern

ring-billed gull

American robin

dunlin

sora

laughing gull

rock dove

least tern

American bittern

Yellowlegs sandpipers skip across the top of the mudflats. They chase insects on long legs and wide feet, or they pick for worms, snails, and fish with their pointy beaks. They don't mind the trains and planes, as long as the Meadowlands provides them with enough food.

least sandpiper

Wilson's phalarope

bobolink

English sparrow

bufflehead

green-winged teal

American wigeon

canvasback

northern pintail

wood duck

Before the mudflats begin to dry out, the tide rolls back in to cover them up again. A ruddy duck's nest, floating on the water, rises with it. Woven into plants growing in the water and riding on the tide, the nest always stays hidden. A silky lining of feathers keeps eggs safe and ducklings warm. Stiff, dry reed stems form sturdy walls.

greater scaup

blue-winged teal

pied-billed grebe

American black duck

barn swallow

double-crested cormorant

lesser scaup

northern shoveler

gadwall

mallard

The mother ruddy duck likes a spot with crowded reeds, just off the shore and out of reach of raccoons that might steal her eggs. There are places for all kinds of homes scattered among the railroads and parking lots. With less pollution and new food sources, the Meadowlands is attracting more birds back to its wetlands.

common goldeneye

hooded merganser

common moorhen

American coot

rough-legged hawk

Canada goose

yellow-crowned night heron

barn owl

snowy egret

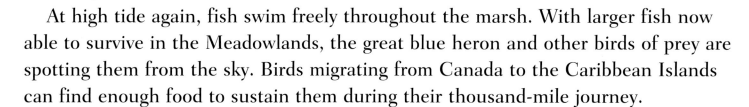

turkey vulture

At high tide again, fish swim freely throughout the marsh. With larger fish now able to survive in the Meadowlands, the great blue heron and other birds of prey are spotting them from the sky. Birds migrating from Canada to the Caribbean Islands can find enough food to sustain them during their thousand-mile journey.

green heron

northern goshawk

merlin

red-tailed hawk

bald eagle

great egret

northern harrier

glossy ibis

peregrine falcon

cattle egret

Most birds of prey that lived here until the 1940s disappeared when pesticides weakened the shells of their eggs and there were too few trees for building nests. They have now slowly returned, thanks to the Meadowlands' most powerful species—humans.

black-crowned night heron

short-eared owl

American kestrel

Cooper's hawk

Tyler

Meera

Javier

Vittorio

Kamila

People in the Meadowlands have changed their views of their habitat. Karin is on a field trip with her class to a salt marsh. With her dip net, she catches three mummichogs and ten grass shrimp. She learns that the variety of life in a salt marsh supports the world's fish and birds. She learns that marsh algae and plants clean water and add oxygen to the air for humans.

Bernadette

Steve

Kerry

Mayra

Peter

Leticia

Arvin

Susan

Bill

Kristin

Karin's teacher explains the other ways marshes help humans, like soaking up floodwater and keeping soil from washing away. Karin also learns how to take care of the wetlands. When she gets home, she'll recycle more and use less of everything, so less waste is dumped in wetlands. She'll teach her family to conserve energy to create less air pollution.

DeShaun

James

Lisette

Seung-Hyun

red-tailed hawk

tree of heaven

freight train

bufflehead

muskrat

Leticia

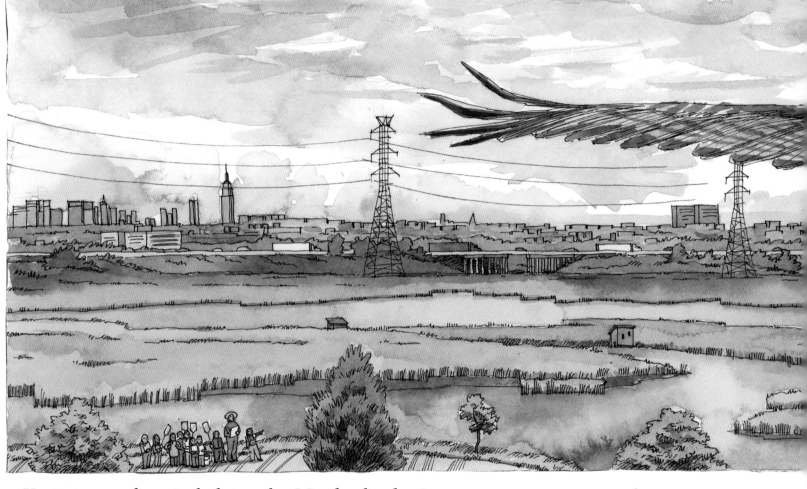

Karin is not alone in helping the Meadowlands. Activists raise awareness about pollution and development of the wetlands. Federal, state, and local governments force polluters to clean up their mistakes and help restore wetlands. Businesses use cleaner manufacturing methods and sponsor conservation efforts. Volunteers clean up garbage and create friendly places for animals, like nest boxes, to attract them back to the marsh.

salt-marsh cordgrass

motorboat

alewife

candy wrapper

blue crab

benzene

swamp mosquito

pumpkinseed

DeShaun

snowy egret

In July 2007, for the first time in fifty years, a young osprey—a bird of prey—leaped out and took flight from a nest its parents had built in the Meadowlands. If a fragile family of ospreys can survive among these reeds and highways, other creatures can return and survive, too. The Meadowlands is recovering, and it is inspiring people in urban wetlands all over the world to look for hope in this flat, wet, beautiful place.

twelve-spotted skimmer

commuter bus

American bittern

condominium

AUTHOR'S NOTE

The history of the Meadowlands began around 13,000 B.C.E., when the Wisconsin Glacier retreated and formed Glacial Lake Hackensack. Between 8,000 and 6,000 B.C.E., the lake broke through a wall of debris left behind by the glacier and drained into the sea, forming the Hackensack River. The river's estuary extended from a point just north of where Overpeck Creek drains into the Hackensack River southward to where the Hackensack River meets the Passaic River and drains into Newark Bay. At its formation, the estuary contained over 20,000 acres of alder and birch swamps, eventually transforming into Atlantic white-cedar swamps, bogs, and freshwater and brackish meadows as the sea level rose.

The first Paleo-Indians probably arrived between 10,000 and 8,000 B.C.E. The first European settlers arrived in the early 1600s. Over 400 years, they logged the Meadowlands' forests for lumber and fuel, drained it for farming and mosquito control, dammed it for drinking water, filled it for building, and cut off its tidal flow with highways and railroads. They also dumped garbage, sewage, and toxic waste in the river and its tributaries. The State of New Jersey created the Hackensack Meadowlands Development Commission in 1969 to clean up pollution in the area and attract businesses. The state roughly defined the Meadowlands District as bounded by Teterboro Airport on the north, the Kearny rail yards on the south, Route 17 on the west, and Routes 1 and 9 on the east. These borders excluded parts of the original Hackensack meadows already developed beyond remediation.

Since the 1980s, activist groups such as Hackensack Riverkeeper, New Jersey Audubon Society, Ducks Unlimited, and NY/NJ Baykeeper have raised public awareness and fought for environmental preservation. In 2001, the U.S. Fish & Wildlife Service established the Hackensack Meadowlands Initiative to protect the ecosystem, and the HMDC changed its name to the New Jersey Meadowlands Commission and began to focus more on conservation.

The Meadowlands District is now thirty square miles of businesses, transportation, and housing, as well as the remaining 8,400 acres of open space, wetlands, and waterways. It is shared by fourteen municipalities, three professional sports teams, three Superfund sites, forty-five species of fish, and 332 species of birds.

Selected Bibliography

Cherry, Lynne. *A River Ran Wild: An Environmental History*. San Diego: Harcourt Brace & Company, 1992.

Conniff, Richard. "Swamps of Jersey: The Meadowlands." *National Geographic*, February 2001.

Kiviat, Erik, and Kristi MacDonald-Beyers. *The Hackensack Meadowlands: A Metropolitan Wildlife Refuge*. Edited by Karen Moore and Carolyn Summers. Lyndhurst, N.J.: Hackensack Conservation Trust, 2006.

Quinn, John R. *Fields of Sun and Grass: An Artist's Journal of the New Jersey Meadowlands*. New Brunswick, N.J.: Rutgers University Press, 1997.

U.S. Fish and Wildlife Service New Jersey Field Office. "The Hackensack Meadowlands Initiative: Preliminary Conservation Planning for the Hackensack Meadowlands Hudson and Bergen Counties, New Jersey." U.S. Fish and Wildlife Service. www.fws.gov/northeast/njfieldoffice/PCP_2007/Hack_Meadow_Initiative_PCP_MAR2007.pdf (March 2007).

Selected Web Sites

Hackensack Riverkeeper: www.hackensackriverkeeper.org

Meadowlands Environment Center: www.rst2.edu/meadowlands/index.shtml

Meadowlands Regional Chamber of Commerce: www.meadowlands.org

National Wetlands Research Center: www.nwrc.usgs.gov

New Jersey Meadowlands Commission: www.njmeadowlands.gov

Wild New Jersey: www.wildnj.com

Photo of ospreys in a nesting platform courtesy of and printed with permission from PSEG, taken by Mark Lovretin